Bipolar Disorder
Understanding Symptoms Mood Swings & Treatment

Anthony Wilkenson

How to deal with a loved one with bipolar

Copyright © dsk-enterprise Inc Ltd. 2014
All rights reserved. No part of this publication may be reproduced in any form without written consent of the author and the publisher. The information contained in this book may not be stored in a retrieval system, or transmitted in any form by any means, electronic, mechanical, photocopying or otherwise without the written permission of the publisher. This book may not be resold, hired out or otherwise disposed by way of trade in any form of binding or cover other than that in which it is published, without the written consent of the publisher.

Legal Disclaimer

The information contained in this book is strictly for educational purpose only. The content of this book is the sole expression and opinion of its author, and not necessarily that of the publisher. It is not intended to cure, treat, and diagnose any kind of disease or medical condition. It is sold with the understanding that the publisher is not rendering any type of medical, psychological, legal, or any other kind of professional advice. You should seek the services of a competent professional before applying concepts in this book. Neither the publisher nor the individual author(s) shall be liable for any physical, psychological, emotional, financial, or commercial damages, directly or indirectly by the use of this material, which is provided "as is", and without warranties. Therefore, if you wish to apply ideas contained in this book, you are taking full responsibility for your actions

Table of Contents

1: Bipolar Disorder Explained
2: Bipolar types and symptoms
3: Causes of bipolar disorder
4: Tests and diagnosis of bipolar
5: Bipolar disorder treatment
6: Overcoming Bipolar Suicidal Thoughts
7: How Meditation Helps Bipolar
8: Stopping the Downward Spiral of Bipolar
9: Bipolar Disorder and Substance Abuse
10: The Impact of Nutrition on Bipolar
11: Help and support
Conclusion

Important Insight

You are about to discover proven steps and strategies on how to properly support and care for a loved one with bipolar disorder. More often than not, people whose loved one has been diagnosed with bipolar disorder wonder what to expect and how they should show their love and support the best way they can. It can be very difficult for those who are diagnosed with bipolar to accept their condition.

In the same way, it can also be overwhelming and at the same time frightening for the family and friends of people with bipolar disorder, especially if they do not know the appropriate ways of supporting and dealing with the condition.

Bipolar disorder, which is also known as manic depression, is a type of mental or psychiatric disorder that is marked by extreme mood swings. Although there have been continuous research and studies on the condition, its ultimate cause remains unknown. On the other hand, some of the presumed contributors to bipolar disorder include brain chemistry, genetics and life events.

All people experience various events in their daily lives. However, people who are suffering due to bipolar disorder experience more persistent episodes of life's "ups and downs," that affect their ability to function as an individual. Bipolar disorder can affect one's thoughts, moods and behavior.

In recent studies, mental health experts estimate that over 2 million adults are afflicted with bipolar disorder. Thus, if you or a loved one has been diagnosed with this condition, the most important step to discard uncertainty is education. Educating yourself about bipolar can help you deal with a loved one who has been inflicted with this unfortunate condition.

1: Bipolar Disorder Explained

Bipolar disorder is a mental condition, which can affect thoughts, moods and behavior of an individual, characterized by extreme mood swings. If you or a loved one has bipolar disorder, then you are most likely to experience episodes of depression and mania. When you are experiencing depression, you will feel lethargic and very low. Hypomania is a less severe type of mania, which can also be experienced by an individual with bipolar disorder.

Bipolar disorder symptoms depend on the mood that an individual experiences. The mood swings endured by an individual with bipolar can last for several days, sometimes months although in some cases, a bipolar may not experience "normal" moods at all.

The first to be diagnosed in bipolar disorder is its depression phase. More often than not, the initial diagnosis would be clinical depression prior to having manic periods at a later time. Afterwards, the diagnosis may be changed to bipolar disorder.

In the depression phase of bipolar, an individual may be overwhelmed with feelings of insignificance or unimportance, leading to suicidal thoughts and other harmful ideas. In the event that you or a loved feels this way or are having severe symptoms of depression, it is best to contact a doctor, local mental health services or care coordinators.

On the other hand, in the manic phase of bipolar disorder, an individual may feel extremely happy about things in their life and have numerous elaborate ideas and plans. They may possibly ignore hunger or sleep, talk fast and become irritable during the manic phase. In addition, they may also tend to spend huge amounts of money on things that are not usually important or affordable.

Furthermore, during the manic phase of bipolar disorder, an individual may perceive mania as a positive feeling, even using it to be extremely creative. Conversely, person who is bipolar may also display psychosis symptoms, which are characterized by seeing or hearing things that do not exist or are not there at all.

The low (depression) and high (mania) phases of bipolar disorder are usually extreme that they can affect an individual's daily life. On the other hand, there are various ways for treating the condition, which are often aimed to control the effects of a phase, as well as support an individual with the disorder in living normally as much as possible.

Many doctors and health experts believe that bipolar disorder can be treated best by using treatments that are combined together. Some of the treatments for bipolar disorder can include medication that treats the primary symptoms of depression and mania as they transpire; medication known as mood stabilizers that prevents episodes of depression, mania, or hypomania and are taken on a long-term basis daily; psychological treatment that helps an individual to deal with depression and provides advice on how to work on relationships; determining the factors that trigger the occurrence of depression or mania; and lifestyle advice that provides help for improving diet, sleep and physical health in general, including doing regular exercise and activities that an individual enjoys and wants to achieve.

Support groups, charities and other related associations often provide support and advice for people with bipolar disorder along with their family, friends and/or caregivers. This support includes self-management and self-help advice specifically on living with the condition on a long-term basis.

Meanwhile, as mentioned earlier, the cause of bipolar disorder is still unknown although health experts think of several factors that trigger an episode. These include genetic, chemical factors, life-changing events and overwhelming problems.

Bipolar disorder is comparatively common across the globe. In fact, 1 out of 100 individuals is diagnosed with it. It can occur regardless of age although it is more common between ages of 18 and 24. Both men and women are likely to develop this condition.

It should also be noted that the mood swing patterns of bipolar disorder are different from one individual to another. For instance, an individual may experience several episodes in his/her lifetime while the other may only have a couple of episodes and are generally stable in between those episodes.

2: Bipolar Disorder Types and Symptoms

Types of Bipolar Disorder

Bipolar disorder is characterized by mood swings that range from extreme highs (manic phase) to extreme lows (depression phase). These episodes can last for several weeks or months.

Bipolar disorder has several subtypes, which have different symptom patterns. The types of bipolar disorder include Bipolar I disorder, Bipolar II disorder, and Cyclothymic disorder.

In ***Bipolar I disorder***, the mood swings can cause substantial challenges in an individual's work and/or relationships. It is often characterized by severe and dangerous episodes of mania.

In ***Bipolar II disorder***, an individual can carry out normal daily activities as it is said to be less severe compared to Bipolar I disorder. Although an individual may experience changes in the way he/she functions due to irritability or elevated mood, he/she can still go on with daily activities. Bipolar II disorder is characterized by hypomania, which is a form of mania that is less severe. Thus, the episodes of depression in Bipolar II disorder is shorter compared to those that occur in Bipolar I.

In *Cyclothymic disorder*, the episodes of depression and hypomania can be disruptive although this type of bipolar disorder is mild compared to the other forms. Cyclothymic disorder is also referred to cyclothymia in which the high and low episodes are less severe.

Symptoms of Bipolar Disorder

The symptoms of bipolar disorder are different from one individual to another. Some individuals may experience depression as the root cause of most of their problems while others may find mania as their primary concern. On the other hand, an individual may experience the symptoms of both depression and mania or hypomania at the same time. This is referred to as mixed episode.

During the depression phase of bipolar disorder, the symptoms can include:
hopelessness, anxiety, sleep problems, fatigue, sadness, suicidal thoughts/behavior, guilt, low/increased appetite, loss of interest in once enjoyed activities, irritability, frequent absences from work/school, poor performance at

work/school, problems in concentration and chronic pain without known cause.

During the manic or hypomanic phase of bipolar disorder, the symptoms can include:

inflated self-esteem, rapid speech, euphoria, poor judgment, aggressive behavior, increased physical activity, racing thoughts, irritation/agitation, risky behavior, increased drive to achieve or perform goals, decreased need for rest/sleep, making unwise financial choices, increased sex drive, careless use of alcohol/drugs, easily distracted, delusions from reality, frequent absences from work/school and poor performance at work/school.

There are other symptoms of bipolar disorder that can be associated with both depression and manic phases. These include seasonal changes in mood, rapid cycling bipolar disorder and psychosis.

Just like seasonal affective disorder (SAD), some individuals with bipolar disorder may have seasonal changes in mood. This means that their moods change depending on the season. For instance, during spring or summer, some individuals may become manic or hypomanic and changes altogether to being depressed during winter or fall. Other individuals experience a reversed cycle where they become depressed during spring or summer and manic or hypomanic during winter or fall.

Some individuals with bipolar disorder experience rapid cycling bipolar disorder or rapid mood shifts. This is characterized by having 4 or more mood swings in a year. The mood shifts for some individuals occur more quickly, even transpiring within hours.

Symptoms of psychosis, which are associated with detachment from reality, may be noticeable during severe episodes of depression or mania. These include hearing or seeing things that are not existing (hallucination) and false but strongly held beliefs (delusions).

Meanwhile, the symptoms of bipolar disorder in children and adolescents can include rapid mood shifts, aggression, explosive temper and reckless behavior. The symptoms are not definitively associated with depression or mania or hypomania.

The mood swings in children and adolescents occur far too quickly as compared to shifts in adults. In fact, the mood swings can occur in within hours, sometimes less. A child or adolescent may experience intense episodes of silliness, giddiness, outbursts, crying, and explosive temper in just a single day.

If you or a loved one is experiencing symptoms of either depression or mania, it is highly advisable to consult a mental health provider or doctor. You should know that bipolar disorder cannot be treated on its own. Treatment from health experts is extremely important in order to control the symptoms of the condition.

Unfortunately, most people with bipolar disorder do not get the treatment that they need. One of the main reasons for this is because many individuals with bipolar disorder do not acknowledge the fact that their extreme mood swings already affect or disrupt their daily lives, as well as the lives of the people close to them.

Some individuals with bipolar disorder even enjoy having the feeling of euphoria, thinking that they are more productive that way. On the other hand, euphoria always leads to emotional crash, leaving an individual worn out and depressed.

If you or a loved is hesitant to seek treatment from health experts, then it is best to confide to a family member, friend, faith leader or anybody whom you trust. They may be the ones to take the first crucial steps for successful bipolar disorder treatment for you or a loved one.

If you or a loved one has suicidal behavior and thoughts, which is common in individuals with bipolar disorder, it is best to get help as soon as possible. You can start by contacting a family member or close friend; consulting a doctor or mental health provider; calling the suicide hotline number; or consulting a spiritual leader, minister, or anybody from a faith community.

If nobody close to you is available to help, it is time to call your local emergency number as soon as you think of inflicting harm on yourself or attempting suicide. If a loved one is considering hurting himself/herself, you should ensure that someone remains with him/her while you call for emergency help.

3: Causes of Bipolar Disorder

In the previous chapters, it has been mentioned that the exact cause of bipolar disorder is not yet known or fully discerned. Most mental health experts believe that there are several factors that act together, leading to the development of the condition in an individual. These causes of bipolar disorder are said to be a complex combination of environmental, physical, and social factors.

Genetics

One of the causes of bipolar disorder is thought to be associated with genetics. The condition seems to be hereditary or run in families. This means that family members of an individual with bipolar disorder are likely to develop the condition themselves. Bipolar disorder cannot be attributed to just a single gene. Mental health experts claim that the condition is triggered by a combination of genetic and environmental factors and not by a single gene per se.

Chemical Imbalance in the Brain

More often than not, mental health experts regard the cause of bipolar disorder to chemical imbalances in the brain. Neurotransmitters or the chemicals that control the brain's functions go through certain imbalances, resulting to symptoms of bipolar disorder. Some of the neurotransmitters that may go through imbalances include serotonin, dopamine and norepinephrine.

When an imbalance in one or more levels of neurotransmitters occurs, it is likely to display symptoms of bipolar disorder. For instance, during an episode of mania, the level of norepinephrine may be too high while during an episode of depression, the level may be too low.

Stressful Triggers

The symptoms of bipolar disorder are often triggered by stressful events including a breakdown of a relationship, death of a family member, friend, or loved one, or physical, emotional, or sexual abuse. These life-changing events can be stressful triggers to an individual and can cause episodes of depression all through the individual's life.

In addition, physical illness, overwhelming problems and sleep disturbances can also trigger the symptoms of bipolar disorder. These include problems or illness associated with work, relationships, and money among others.

4: Tests and Diagnosis of Bipolar Disorder

Initial Assessment with GP

If you or a loved one has been suspected to have bipolar disorder, general practitioners (GP) will generally refer you to a specialist such as a psychiatrist or qualified mental health expert. In the event that you or a loved one has the tendency to inflict harm on yourself or anyone else, the GP will quickly arrange an appointment for you with the specialist.

Assessment with a Specialist

Once you or your loved one has been arranged an appointment, the psychiatrist will lay several questions that would discern if you or a loved one has bipolar disorder. The treatments will be determined accordingly.

During the assessment with the psychiatrist, you or your loved one will be asked about the symptoms experience, as well as when they first occurred, and about your usual feelings that lead to an episode of depression or mania. The psychiatrist will also ask about any suicidal thought or behavior that you or your loved one might have.

In this assessment, the psychiatrist aims to determine both family and medical background so that he/she would know if any relative also has or had the condition. In the event that you have a relative who has bipolar disorder, the psychiatrist is likely to talk to that individual, although your permission may be asked prior to doing so.

Other Tests

You may need to undergo other tests to discern if you have a physical problem such as overactive or underactive thyroid. Undergoing some other tests may depend on the symptoms of bipolar disorder.

Advanced Directives

Upon diagnosis of bipolar disorder, it is necessary to speak with the psychiatrist regarding the condition specifically about the treatment and care that you or your loved one needs. Conversely, there are some cases in which an individual may not be in the position to make decisions for him/her regarding the care or treatment needed. This is specifically true if the symptoms are severe. In this case, they may need an *advanced directive*, which is a set of instructions that are written in advance and state the treatments, care, and support that an individual wants or do not want in cases when the person is unable to decide at a later stage.

5: Bipolar Disorder Treatment

In most cases, bipolar patients need lifelong treatment even if they experience periods of relief. A psychiatrist or an equally qualified mental health expert usually administers treatment for bipolar disorder.

It is also possible that an individual with the condition may avail the services of a treatment team, which involves psychologists, psychiatric nurses, and social workers. Some of the common primary treatments for bipolar disorder include medications, education and support groups, and individual, family, or group psychotherapy or psychological counseling.

If you or your loved one has the tendency to inflict harm on themselves or become detached from reality, the psychiatrist or doctor may recommend having you hospitalized. The initial treatment for bipolar usually involve taking medication for balancing individual's moods. As soon as the symptoms are controlled, the psychiatrist may advise the most appropriate long-term treatment for the individual with bipolar disorder.

Maintenance or continued treatment is usually utilized for managing long-term bipolar.

Individuals with the condition who tend to miss out on their maintenance treatment are likely to have minor changes in moods that can turn to full-blown depression or mania. Some individuals who skip treatment are also at high risk of symptom relapse.

An individual with an alcohol or drug problem may also need to have substance abuse treatment in order to manage or control the symptoms of bipolar disorder.

Medications

Bipolar disorder can be treated using a number of medications. If one kind of medication does not work, other types may be tried until the most efficient type or combination of types are discerned. More often than not, psychiatrists and doctors suggest combining medications in order to come up with optimal results. Medications for bipolar usually include mood stabilizers and those that help in reducing or discarding anxiety and depression. Mood stabilizers are used to prevent episodes of highs (mania) and lows (depression).

Some of the most common medications for bipolar disorder include lithium, anticonvulsants, antipsychotics, antidepressants, symbyax, and benzodiazepines.

Lithium

This is an efficient mood stabilizer that prevents episodes of highs and lows for specific levels or degrees of bipolar. It has been used for a number of years although periodic blood tests are usually required when using lithium as medication. This is because immoderate use of lithium may result to kidney and thyroid problems. Some common side effects of lithium include dry mouth, digestive problems and restlessness.

Anticonvulsants

Anticonvulsants are also mood stabilizers that help in treating mixed episodes of highs and lows. The most common anticonvulsants include divalproex (Depakote), valproic acid (Stavzor or Depakene), asenapine (Saphris), and lamotrigine (Lamictal). The side effects of anticonvulsants vary depending on the type of medication although some of the common side effects include drowsiness, dizziness and weight gain. In rare cases, anticonvulsants may result to blood disorders, liver problems or skin rashes.

Antipsychotics

Antipsychotics are usually taken if anticonvulsants do not have an effect on an individual with bipolar disorder. Some antipsychotic medications include quetiapine (Seroquel), aripiprazole (Abilify), risperidone (Risperdal), and olanzapine (Zyprexa). The U.S. Food and Drug Administration (FDA) had approved only one antipsychotic medication for bipolar disorder treatment. This is quetiapine. Conversely, psychiatrists and doctors are still allowed to prescribe other types of medications for bipolar disorder referred to as off-label use.

The side effects of antipsychotic medications vary although the most common include sleepiness, blurred vision, weight gain, rapid heartbeat and tremors. In some cases, using antipsychotic medications may affect attention and memory, as well as result to involuntary body or facial movements. Children who take antipsychotics for bipolar treatment usually experience weight gain, which is still a pending concern for many doctors.

Antidepressants

Antidepressants are usually taken with mood stabilizers for treating bipolar because they can trigger episodes of highs (mania). The most common side effects of antidepressants include reduced sexual drive/desire and problems on reaching orgasm. Similarly, older versions of antidepressants such as MAO inhibitors and tricyclics can result to harmful side effects and call for thorough monitoring.

Symbyax

Symbyax is a combination of the antipsychotic olanzapine and the antidepressant fluoxetine. This medication helps in treating depression and is also considered a mood stabilizer. The FDA has approved Symbyax only for treating bipolar disorder. Some of the known side effects of Symbyax include increased appetite, weight gain and drowsiness. In some cases, it can also cause sexual problems as that of antidepressants.

Benzodiazepines

Benzodiazepines are anti-anxiety medications that help improve sleep and reduce anxiety. They are used for relieving anxiety but only for a short period. Some of the most common benzodiazepines include lorazepam (Ativan), chlordiazepoxide (Librium, clonazepam (Klonopin), alprazolam (Zanax and Niravam, and diazepam (Valium). The side effects of these medications can include problems with memory and balance, drowsiness and reduced coordination of muscles.

Determining the Right Medication

It may take a little trial and error to be able to determine the right medication for you or a loved one with bipolar. Finding the right medication necessitates patience given that some medications may only take full effect after a few weeks or months. In general, a psychiatrist or doctor changes only one medication at a time in order to determine the medication that works in relieving the symptoms of bipolar disorder with the least side effects.

Thus, this can take a few weeks or longer. In some instances, a psychiatrist or doctor may be prompted to adjust your medication specifically if the symptoms change. Once the right medication and its doses are determined, the side effects will already be bearable as the body amends to the medications.

There are several bipolar disorder medications that can be linked with birth defects specifically if the individual with bipolar takes them while pregnant. As such, health experts suggest that women with bipolar disorder take or use efficient contraception or birth control pills/methods in order to prevent pregnancy.

It is best that these women discuss their options with their doctors because birth control medications may become less efficient when taken with some medications for bipolar. Women who plan to get pregnant should consult their doctors regarding their treatment options. If diagnosed with bipolar during or after pregnancy, breast-feeding options should also be discussed given that some medications for the condition can be included in the breast milk and endanger the infant's health.

Psychotherapy

One of the vital parts of treating bipolar disorder is psychotherapy. These include cognitive behavioral therapy, psycho-education, family therapy, group therapy and other therapies.

Cognitive behavioral therapy

Cognitive behavioral therapy is the most common type of individual therapy used for bipolar disorder. The priority of this therapy is to determine unhealthy, negative behaviors and beliefs and replace them with positive ones. Cognitive behavioral therapy can be very efficient in identifying the triggers of bipolar. It also involves efficient strategies in coping with upsetting events and managing stress.

Psycho-education

Psycho-education involves counseling in order to help individuals with bipolar learn and understand their condition. It usually encourages the patient to participate in the counseling together with their family or loved ones. Both patients and their loved ones will be able to identify warning signs of mood swings and discern the best approach to treat bipolar disorder.

Family therapy

Family therapy as the name implies, involves the individual with bipolar and his/her family seeing a psychologist or qualified mental health specialist. This type of psychotherapy can help in reducing stress within the family of the bipolar. In addition, family therapy can help solve problems, resolve conflicts and communicate better within the family.

Group therapy

Group therapy is a type of psychotherapy that provides a forum for communicating and learning from other bipolar patients. It is also an efficient way to develop better skills in establishing and maintaining relationships.

Other therapies

Other therapies for bipolar disorder have been studied and proven efficient in early detection. Some therapies are also efficient in identifying and resolving problems with an individual's daily routine and improving social and personal relationships.

Electroconvulsive Therapy (ECT)

Electroconvulsive therapy (ECT) is an efficient treatment for individuals with bipolar episodes of severe depression. It is also considered the best alternative treatment for those who do not see improvements or reduction of their symptoms from other types of treatment. ECT involves the use of electrical currents, which pass through the brain.

Although researchers are uncertain of how ECT works, it is believed that electric shock may effect changes in the brain chemistry, leading to mood improvements. ECT may be the best option if an individual with bipolar experience severe depression or mania. It is also a good idea for pregnant women who are not allowed to take regular medications. But be aware, ECT can cause confusion and temporary memory loss.

Transcranial Magnetic Stimulation

Transcranial magnetic stimulation is a type of bipolar treatment that involves the application of rapid pulses of magnetic field to the head. Like ECT, researchers are uncertain of how rapid pulses help in treating bipolar although it has been proven to have an antidepressant effect. Conversely, not all individuals with bipolar disorder can be treated with this therapy. It is also unclear who are specifically qualified to undergo this therapy.

Treatment for Children and Adolescents with Bipolar Disorder

Although children and adolescents with bipolar are treated in the same way as adults do, the safety and efficiency of medications in children are still not guaranteed. This is because most of the medications and treatments for bipolar disorder are based on adult research.

The treatments for bipolar are decided depending on the severity or degree of the condition, the exact symptoms, side effects of medications, and other factors. ECT may be used for adolescents with severe Bipolar I disorder.

More often than not, psychiatrist and doctors require children with bipolar disorder to go through counseling as a preliminary treatment and to avoid relapse of symptoms. Psychotherapy is one of the most efficient treatments for children and adolescents as it involves teachers and school counselors who are responsible for helping children address learning difficulties, develop coping skills and resolve interpersonal problems.

Psychotherapy is also efficient in building stronger family bonds and improving communication within the family. Adolescents with bipolar disorder who are likewise involved in substance abuse may also need psychotherapy.

6: Overcoming Bipolar Suicidal Though

Suicidal thoughts are common with people who suffer from mental illness, depression and most certainly bipolar disorder. Even if these individuals do not end up committing suicide, the mere thought of suicide does not bring any good to the individual. It can be tormenting and in extreme cases it can lead you to a downward spiral of depression.

It is therefore very important as a bipolar individual to learn how to manage your thought processes effectively to avoid the suicidal mentality.

The Beginning of the Suicidal Thought Pattern

Suicidal thoughts begin with small things such as intolerable loneliness, crushing depression and feelings of worthlessness. Just as individuals are different, so are their suicidal thought cycles. One bipolar individual will go through a slightly different suicidal thought cycle triggered by different thoughts.

Regardless of your individual uniqueness, whenever you feel like committing suicide as a result of bipolar, there are some things that you can do to stop this.

Techniques for Dealing with Suicidal Thoughts

Thought Stopping

One of the powerful ways of nipping suicidal thoughts in the bud is to stop them. In reality, this technique may be more difficult to accomplish. However, the moment a suicidal thought finds its way into your brain, you need to authoritatively tell it to stop. Some people say this aloud while others just murmur in silence but the bottom line is that you need to say this verbally in order to stop the thought.

By doing this, you are breaking free from the jinx of the suicidal thought pattern.

Thought Switching

This is closely related to the thought stopping technique but it is more of a progression. Here, you switch your thoughts to something else that is more pleasurable and constructive as a way of delinking yourself from the suicidal thought pattern. It helps if you start plotting scenarios that you enjoy thinking about such as taking a vacation, gardening or going for a leisure walk. This will relieve you and make it easier for you to transit from thinking about suicide to thinking about the beauty of life.

Distracting Your Thought Pattern by Engaging in an Activity

People who are deep into suicidal thoughts usually do not want to engage in anything because they feel totally helpless and hopeless. It takes commitment and energy to distract your thoughts by engaging in an activity such as organizing your book shelf, playing fetch with your pet or even cleaning out the refrigerator. Any activity that will emotionally transfer your thoughts from one point to another is good.

Give Yourself Time

Thoughts are never permanent and with time, they pass. This is true even for suicidal thoughts. All you need is patience. However, you need to be aware prior to getting into this cycle of thoughts that it will not last forever. Also, you must not dwell on those thoughts because this will give them emotional muscles making them to linger a little bit longer before finally passing out. By being patient, you need to understand that episodes of sadness will come and go. Meanwhile, you must learn to withstand them.

Get Help from Family, Friends and Professionals

No man is an island and each one of us needs every one of us and every one of us needs each one of us. Even if you are certain beyond reasonable doubt that your suicidal thought pattern will not lead you to actual suicide, you need to leverage on the power of friends and family.

Talking to them can help you in opening up other perspectives that you had earlier closed doors to. Whatever dark your feelings are, talking them over with a circle of friends or very close family members will make them seem less dark. The affirmations of love and care that you will hear from these people will give you a reason why you should live another day.

Professional assistance in form of counseling is highly encouraged at this stage. Suicidal thoughts are not a small thing to be ignored but rather should be given the attention that they deserve so that they can be uprooted at the earliest possible stage. The professional will be able to access you and using his experience and skills, he will prescribe treatment should it be necessary.

Resist the Urge to Suicidal Thoughts

Resistance is a personal initiative that you have to undertake. Remember, every individual including those with bipolar disorder have reasons for living. Some of them want to live so that they can see their children grow up. Others want to make it to the best colleges and pursue the career of their dreams, and still others want to live so that they can enjoy the goodness of this life. Every person has a different list of reasons as to why they want to live.

In order to successfully resist suicidal thoughts, you need to make your list in advance while you are not thinking about suicide. List down all the things that make you want to see the following day. This is the same list that you will have to refer to the moment your bipolar has led you into a suicidal thought pattern.

Learn how to differentiate between your illness and you. The part of you that is driving you down the suicidal path is your bipolar and not you. The moment you make this distinction, you will comfortably sail through by confronting your illness and making positive affirmations that you shall live and not die.

Developing a resistance to suicidal thoughts is not an overnight affair and as such you need to be patient and consistent. Start small and you will soon find out that you have developed such a huge wall that will give you enough resistance against such thoughts.

7: How Meditation Helps Bipolar

Meditation is an age old practice that has been used as a component of many holistic healing processes all over the globe. Depending on the region, this practice has adopted different names, the most famous of which is yoga. The intensity of meditation and the fact that it engages the entire brain faculty helps in stabilizing moods in bipolar disorder individuals.

Contrary to popular belief, bipolar is more than just mood swing. The individuals go through dramatic life experiences shifting from mania to depression and this makes it difficult for them to live a normal life. There are ways in which meditation can help in calming and neutralizing bipolar disorders.

Meditation Helps in Equalizing Unbalanced Moods

Mood swings is the common condition that characterizes bipolar individuals. Through meditation, these individuals can start experiencing a greater sense of calmness and peace. In addition, meditation helps in leveling their moods for considerable periods of time after the meditation session.

Daily meditation routine has been found through research and study to be effective in raising the mental awareness of the individual. This prevents them from either getting to high or too low by helping them to maintain an advanced and well balanced state of mind. Many bipolar individuals introduced into the meditation program have been able to successfully fight the urge for self medication.

Helps in Boosting Brain Neurotransmitters

Bipolar medication is usually administered with the intention of boosting the brain neurotransmitter chemicals thereby reducing mood swings and enhancing the state of the mind. Meditation is a proven method that works in similar fashion as bipolar medication in boosting the neurotransmitters.

The most important brain chemicals are dopamine, serotonin and GABA. There are instances when these chemicals become insufficient in the brain thus impacting on the overall mental health including the mood. Routine meditation is very important because it does not involve any pills and yet it can increase the mood elevating chemicals in the brain. This partially explains why in some of the bipolar treatment programs, meditation is included as a supplement to enhance the healing process.

Gives You Control over Your Mind

Meditation is the single most effective way through which you can take control over your mind and distance it from the happenings around you. Bipolar individuals usually struggle with mood swings because their entire being is linked to their state of mind. Whenever they feel low, then everything else surrounding them is negative.

Meditation comes in as a powerful tool that helps them to detach naturally from their particular states of mind and take control of their thinking and feelings. Meditation puts the power to decide on their destiny right before their eyes. As a treatment and recovery procedure, meditation therefore can help bipolar individuals to stabilize very fast.

Activates Brain's Prefrontal Cortex

The prefrontal cortex is the command center of the entire brain system. It is the custodian of judgment, and as such can differentiate between what is right from wrong and good from bad. The orchestration of thoughts and the outcome of actions are exclusively determined within this region.

Meditation activates this area making you more alert and sober in your decision making, perspectives and self perception.

Because bipolar disorder snowballs into personality issues, having access to these control center of the brain can effectively give you the reigns to determine the various states of mind. Scientific researches and studies have concluded that meditation enhances this region of the brain and evens out the manic as well as deactivating any depression tendencies.

Habitual Meditation Enhances Internal Skill Development

The overall goal of meditation is to help you live a normal life away from distractions. Bipolar disorder individuals, who make it their habit to meditate, will gradually develop a set of skills on their internal system that enables them to switch from one state of the mind to another. For instance, the skills will empower them to move from a state of anxiety and confusion to one of calm and peace of mind. This has made meditation to be the closest cure for individuals suffering from bipolar enabling them to live an ordinary life just like anyone else.

In every way, meditation brings along a truck load of benefits to bipolar patients that have no risks attached. For optimal effectiveness, meditation can be combined with other bipolar prescriptions or therapies.

8: Stopping the Downward Spiral of Bipolar

Depression caused by the bipolar condition can be immobilizing when the condition is chronic. The mood swings that characterize bipolar are closely linked to depression, especially in cases where such mood swings are severe.

The difficulty that some bipolar patients find themselves in is that of differentiating depression due to external factors and that which is caused by bipolar. For instance, if you suffer the loss of a loved one, fail a test or do not make it in time to seize an opportunity, it is common that you will become cold and depressed.

However, this kind of depression is different because it is linked to external factors unlike that of bipolar where the problem is your internal system.

Dysthymia is one of the common types of depression that has less intense symptoms but tends to last longer. Bipolar patients usually suffer this kind of depression which may confine them to a regular moody state for a period of more than two years.

In addition to the moody characteristics, the bipolar patients may also display the following symptoms:

- Concentration, low self-esteem
- Low energy combined with fatigue
- Binge eating or low appetite
- Feeling of helplessness and hopelessness
- Irregular sleeping patterns where the person sleeps for long hours or very few hours

If no attention is given, dysthymia can literally take over your life and rule it. Many people who suffer from depression resort to psychotherapy and anti-depressants medications. These can be life saving and are highly recommended whenever signs of depression start to manifest.

There are several ways you can halt the downward spiral of bipolar depression.

Be Gentle on Yourself

It is common for people with depression to exhibit negativity and blame it on themselves. This position does not help you in fighting depression but rather takes you further down the spiral of depression.

You should understand that bipolar depression is not a character defect but rather a mood disorder that can happen to anyone including you. You should therefore treat yourself gently and never be harsh because this can weaken your resilience to stop the condition.

Assume you are Not Depressed

Because depression is an internal and psychological condition, it needs to be solved using a psychological strategy. One of the ways you can achieve this is by taking a different position from that of depression. For instance, you can smile at people and engage in conversations that are interesting and humorous. This will help you to laugh your condition away thereby offsetting the downward spiral of depression.

Remember, it is not self denial but rather a deliberate move to free yourself from the shackles of depression. When you move around and interact with other people, your mood will change for the better enabling you to cheer up.

Practice Thought Stopping

One of the reasons why the downward spiral of depression gathers momentum really fast is because we tend to feed it with thoughts that are negative and depressing.

By practicing thought stopping, you will be able to identify and arrest negative thoughts before they take toll on you. For some bipolar patients, this would mean talking to themselves whenever a negative thought comes to their mind. Other patients may slap themselves or wear a rubber band that they can snap whenever a negative thought crosses their mind.

Thought stopping is a practice that needs time and consistency if it is to succeed. The more you practice it, the longer it sticks and finally becomes a habit.

Challenge Your Self Perception

As a bipolar patient, you will come across situations that put you down. For instance, you may visualize yourself as being worthless and incapable of achieving much in life. To challenge this thought, you need to change your perception and mindset and accommodate an alternative view that reflects the powerful you.

Whether the negative perception is about family, friends or just about yourself, you need to practice positive perceptions. You will be surprised at how fast you get out of the depression pit. You can play inner attorney and issue a dissenting opinion to the evidence of hopelessness and worthlessness provided by the negative perception.

Question yourself on the role that depression plays within your life. The answers that come from this will help you to realize the beauty of positivity towards family, friends and society.

Look Out for Hobbies that Give You Pleasure

Depression comes in to steal your joy and deprive you of the things that you previously enjoyed. As a matter of fact, you need to be careful the moment you start losing interest on things that you once had fun engaging in.

To avoid descending further down the spiral of depression, you can look out for new hobbies that give you happiness and joy. However small they may be, they can help you in reviving the lost joy and pleasure.

Lightening Dark Moods with Humor

Laughter is the best medicine and panacea to many kinds of illnesses and conditions. Bipolar depression can find its perfect match in humor. Whether you are going to watch comedy or hilarious live shows, you will be able to laugh your depression off and get some relief. Humor gives you a different perspective towards pain and can help you in turning a negative situation into a lighter moment.

Give Yourself Healing Time

Because bipolar depression does not come in a flash, it will also not go away overnight. In fact, tricking yourself into thinking that bipolar depression has an instant miracle is a white lie. You need to be patient and give yourself adequate healing time. You will have to endure the cycles of anger, pain and sadness, but be hopeful that one day you will be free from such conditions. For you to heal, you need to appreciate the part of the healing process which involves acknowledgement of pain and finding joy amidst the instances of pain. This will give you strength to carry on.

Reach Out to Family and Friends

Isolation is never a solution to depression. If anything, the more you seclude yourself, the higher your chances of descending into the bottomless pit of bipolar depression.

It is important that you utilize the bond of family and friends to support yourself until you get back to your feet. In the event of persistent feelings of helplessness, you can seek professional help.

You have to remember that depression is a condition like any other and it is never permanent. It does not matter how long you have been in depression. Like the Phoenix bird, you can rise again from your ashes.

9: Bipolar Disorder and Substance Abuse

Bipolar disorder individuals usually succeed in using a combination of medication and psychotherapy to treat their conditions. However, not everyone responds positively to these curative measures making some individuals to opt for self medication. This attempt to fight bipolar symptoms could be undertaken while the individuals are still on traditional treatment.

There is a high tendency of individuals who have bipolar disorders to suffer drug and substance abuse. There is a link between the two, although scientific research is yet to establish the credibility of the assumptions. Preliminary research has indicated that 6 out of 10 people who suffer bipolar disorders are also engaged in drug abuse. Where bipolar disorder occurs together with substance abuse, the following complications may result.

- Difficulty in diagnosing the bipolar disorder
- Misdiagnosis due to the substance mimicking the symptoms of bipolar disorder
- Adverse effects of the substance on bipolar disorder treatment

There are a number of reasons why bipolar disorder individuals end up in drug and substance abuse. You should note that they do it out of need and not necessarily out of choice. The Reasons for Substance Abuse in Bipolar Disorder Individuals are:

Self Medication

There is a growing urge within bipolar disorder individuals to self medicate their symptoms. This is because they feel self medication will give them the relief that they need and bring back their lives to normal.

Some of the symptoms associated with bipolar disorders such as poor judgment, impulsive behavior and helplessness increase the likelihood for self medication. During the manic phase of bipolar disorder, most individuals feel the urge to engage in pleasurable activities amongst them, the indulgence in drug and alcohol abuse. With time, this can create addiction.

Prior Abuse of Substances

Not all bipolar disorder individuals abuse drugs due to the onset of the condition. Some of them were already engaging in drug and alcohol indulgence even before the symptoms of bipolar disorder appeared.

In some of these cases, the potential for developing bipolar may have already existed, but the symptoms do not come into light until the substance abuse has taken root in the individual. Whenever bipolar disorder and substance abuse are detected together (dual diagnosis), the effectiveness of the treatment administered goes down drastically. Some of these individuals may not even seek treatment after all.

There is a higher risk of substance abuse even in those individuals who suffer episodes of mania instead of full scale depression.

Diagnosis Complications

Whenever bipolar disorder individuals go through phases of depression and periods of mania, they tend to indulge in stimulant drugs that supposedly will help them remain alert and function normally. These drugs which may include amphetamines and cocaine are commonly used to fight the symptoms of depression such as sleep problems, lack of energy and feelings of apathy.

Alcohol is a depressant and this is one of the reasons why bipolar individuals combine it with other depressants in a bid to achieve temporal relief from anxiety, pain, hopelessness and insomnia. The problem comes during diagnosis where an individual who has been using alcohol and other drugs to self medicate causes difficulty in diagnosis as the effects of alcohol may be misinterpreted as those of bipolar disorder.

Any substance whether it is a drug or not that alters the mood or behavior of an individual has the capacity to produce symptoms that resemble those of bipolar. Depending on the history of the patient presented and its accuracy, the physician may not be able to tell with certainty whether it is a bipolar disorder or it is a condition resulting from substance abuse.

Drugs come in two main categories; depressants or stimulants. Depressants work on the body system to eliminate anxiety and tension by causing the body to go into a calmer mood. Stimulants however, increase the energy levels of an individual making them to feel happier and excited.

Upon diagnosis, the effects of alcoholism or substance abuse may be so prominent that the possibility of an underlying bipolar disorder is overruled. The physician will need to undertake a thorough screening so he may be able pinpoint with accuracy the root of the problem.

Research has shown that bipolar individuals who are undiagnosed, and with the combination of alcohol or drugs, chances of misdiagnosis are very high. Because of this, they do not receive accurate treatment and they may finally end up worse than before. When the individuals become sober, chances of the bipolar disorder symptoms becoming evident are very high.

Treatment Issues in Dual Diagnosis

The treatment of bipolar disorder patients who have dual diagnosis is not as effective as those who do not use substances or alcohol for self medication.

Most of the medication used in treating bipolar conditions is mood stabilizers and antipsychotic medications that help in stabilizing the brain chemicals thereby preventing the occurrence of mania. Alcohol and drugs however, disrupts this balance of these chemicals causing the individual to go through a depressive episode despite them taking medication.

It is important to note that bipolar treatment does not solve the primary problem but rather manage the symptoms. Intake of alcohol and drugs worsens the symptoms of bipolar making it very difficult for medication to alleviate them.

The Emergence of Dual Diagnosis Programs

There is no obvious link between substance abuse and psychiatric disorders such as bipolar disorder. Dual diagnosis programs have emerged that offer treatment for both conditions. The programs address fully the substance disorders as well as the psychiatric disorders. According to experts in this field, treatment of bipolar disorder cannot be effective if substance abuse is not addressed comprehensively.

In dual diagnosis programs, the medical and family history of the individual will be analyzed to determine the cause of the disorder. This diagnosis will also shed light on whether the problem is caused by both bipolar and substance abuse problem.

In order for bipolar disorder individuals to live a normal and healthy life, they must be individually treated for both conditions. By visiting dual diagnosis centers, the individuals will be able to secure the treatment that they want while at the same time getting the advantage of receiving all forms of treatment to erase any doubts of dual diagnosis.

10: The Impact of Nutrition on Bipolar

Bipolar individuals experience cyclic mood swings at times lasting for a few minutes. It is common to see such individuals depressed and the next minute they are elated. In many instances, doctors usually prescribe bipolar medication to tame this condition and help in easing other symptoms of bipolar disorder.

Researchers who have concentrated their study on the nutrition side of bipolar treatment have discovered that some foods can either hinder or boost the effects of mood disorders. As a result, these researchers recommended that the treatment of bipolar should include nutritional counseling as well. This will give them a holistic approach to the treatment regime.

According to a research done in the United Kingdom by Wesley Freeman-Smith and Evanne Constantine both of Lewisham Counseling and Counselor Associates, there are specific nutritional guidelines that need to be observed by people suffering from bipolar disorder. The researchers went ahead to make some recommendations on nutrients such as Vitamin B, Omega-3 and magnesium as some of the top supplements to be included in bipolar disorder diet. This is because such foods have an impact on the neurotransmitters in the brain system and this improves moods.

Benefits of Omega-3

Omega-3 fatty acids which are present in fish oil contain components that help in stabilizing the mood and regulate behavioral patterns in people suffering from bipolar disorder. Some of the fish that have high quantities of Omega-3 include tuna, salmon, mackerel, herring and trout. Fish oil supplements are also excellent as Omega-3 sources. Research has shown that fish oil can help in combating depression and this by extension means that Omega-3 will have the ability to reduce the impact of bipolar. In the study, 75 patients were using Omega-3 while the rest were using a placebo. The Omega-3 patients recorded a drastic decrease in instances of depression.

The Impact of a Balanced Diet

According to nutritionist, consuming a balanced diet is important because the body requires the various nutritional components for it to be stable. The fruits, the grains, vegetables, dairy, lean protein and nuts will combine together to provide a great nutritional support to the body system.

Bipolar patients who are on medication should regularly get in touch with the physicians who will give them directions as per the types of foods that they can eat which will not affect their medication program.

Herbal and alcoholic supplements must be avoided at all instances because they act as depressants and can result into substance abuse if taken in excessive quantities. This will make it difficult for the right diagnosis to be done because alcohol and other drugs tend to mimic the symptoms of bipolar disorder.

Foods That Adversely Affect Bipolar Treatment

There are certain foods that should be avoided at all costs for a person suffering from bipolar disorder. This is because they affect the medication by lowering its effectiveness. It should be noted that any foods which negatively react with bipolar treatment should be dropped and not the medication.

Caffeine – Caffeine has been discovered through research to affect the sleeping patterns and mood.

People take caffeine which is contained in coffee to keep themselves alert. While this may seem enjoyable, it can affect your moods and also react negatively with benzodiazepines which are used to treat anxiety and mania.

Salt

While it is necessary to put some salt in your food, you need to be careful that you do not go beyond the normal quantities. For bipolar disorder patients who are under lithium medication, taking foods with so much salt can affect the efficiency of lithium in the body.

Fatty Foods

Whether it is fatty content in meat or in the vegetable oil used in preparing meals, you need to be careful because too much fat will affect some bipolar medications rendering them ineffective.

Grapefruit

However sweet and nutritious they may look, grapefruits can cause problems with bipolar disorder. The grapefruit juice interferes with medication that contains benzodiazepines and anticonvulsants. The interaction between grapefruit and these components can even cause toxicity or impairment.

Tyramine Content

Foods that have tyramine have been associated with high blood pressure especially in bipolar patients who take Monoamine Oxidase (MAO) inhibitors. These inhibitors contain antidepressants such as Parnate and Nardil. Some of the tyramine content foods that may affect these inhibitors include fermented cheese, champagne, bananas, soy sauce and liver.

The management of bipolar disorder therefore involves more than the medication. While it is important to get the right medication, it is also important that you get the right combination of food and nutrients that will go along with the medication. This way, you will be able to achieve an optimal balance and health of mind and body.

11: Support and Help for a Loved One with Bipolar Disorder

In most cases, supporting, helping and/or dealing with an individual with bipolar disorder can be very challenging. Parents, spouses, children and friends of individuals with bipolar disorder are often victims of the condition as well.

If you have a loved one with bipolar disorder, you are most likely to face a difficult situation. However, you cannot blame a loved one for having the effects of the condition; thus, you need to be sympathetic and supportive. There are several things you can do in order to support and help a loved one with bipolar disorder. You do not have to be a professional to care for a loved one with this type of mental condition. All it takes is love, understanding and compassion.

Educate Yourself

The first step that you should take is to read about bipolar. Although your loved one will make you aware of his/her condition, it is still advisable to educate yourself about the symptoms, causes, treatments, triggers and other pertinent information about the disorder. Having knowledge about what you are dealing with can help you understand what your loved one is going through.

Accept the Diagnosis

Bipolar disorder can be controlled by taking medications. However, it cannot be cured totally. Thus, you need to accept the diagnosis laid on your loved one. You should realize that the condition is not always bad as it may seem. Your loved one is still the same person. They just have special needs.

Pay Attention

Making assumptions on what your loved one is going through is not a good idea if you are determined in helping him/her cope with bipolar. You need to listen and pay attention to what your loved one wants to tell you. The emotions and feelings of your loved one should not be treated as symptoms or signs of the disorder. It does not follow that when an individual has bipolar disorder, his/her views are insignificant or invalid.

Identify the Symptoms

More often than not, you may notice mood swings or emotional changes occurring in your loved one before he/she does. It is best to keep track of the symptoms so that you can prevent an episode from pushing through or at least understand the situation of your loved one. Early detection of symptoms can make a huge difference in terms of treatment and caring for the individual with bipolar disorder. Make sure you are not too intrusive that your loved one might suspect that you are spying on them.

Do Things with Your Loved One

Most people with bipolar disorder tend to detach themselves from people, if not, from the world. As such, it is advisable to encourage your loved one to enjoy things that he/she used to do. You may ask your loved one to do things together like taking a walk, dining out, or shopping. However, if your loved one resists, do not try to push the idea. You may try again after a few days just as long as your loved one feels he/she is still a part of your life.

Make Plans

Given that bipolar disorder is an unpredictable mental condition, it is best to make plans specifically for the "bad" times. Plan together with your loved one on what both of you would do if symptoms occur. When both of you agree on what to do and expect from each other, the situation will be much more bearable.

Speak Out Your Concerns

You have all the right to express your own concerns to your loved one with bipolar given that his/her behavior can affect you substantially. However, make sure that you do not give even a small hint of blame to the person. Just focus on how his/her actions make you feel and how such behavior affects you. Generally, it is advised that when you talk about your own concerns, do it with a counselor or therapist.

Know Your Limitations

Although supporting and caring for your loved one is crucial to his/her treatment, you need to remember that you also have your own limitations. You cannot be there for him/her all throughout the day. You might be limited to help your loved one with bipolar due to your work or other personal things that you need to attend to. It is highly recommended to let family members or other people close to you to become involved as well. It is great to help your loved one but you need to know that you also have burdens that you need to address on your own.

Care for Yourself

While you try to take care of your loved one with bipolar, you tend to neglect your own needs. Remember, you need to stay strong and healthy both physically and emotionally so that you can support and care for your loved one optimally.

Pushing yourself too much is not good for anyone given that you would eventually burn out and may not be able to help altogether. Make sure you still give time for yourself, eat healthy and maintain regular exercise. The more you take care of yourself, the more you will be able to support and care for your loved one with bipolar disorder.

Conclusion

I hope this book was able to help you better understand what bipolar disorder is all about. By allowing yourself to be more open to bipolar disorder, you should be able to support, care, and deal with your loved one with this mental condition.

Supporting your loved one with bipolar maybe difficult, but if you let friends and family involved, the key to recovery is much easier.

Finally, if you enjoyed this book, please take the time to share your thoughts and post a review on Amazon. It'd be greatly appreciated. Thank you and good luck!

Printed in Great Britain
by Amazon.co.uk, Ltd.,
Marston Gate.